First published in Great Britain in 2005
by Zero To Ten Limited,
2A Portman Mansions, Chiltern Street,
London W1U 6NR

Copyright © 2005 Zero To Ten Limited
Text copyright © 2005 Meg Clibbon
Illustrations copyright © 2005 Lucy Clibbon

Clibbon, Meg
Imagine you're a cowboy

2. West (U.S.) - Pictorial works - Juvenile literature
I. Title

978

ISBN-10: 1 84089 427 X

13-digit ISBN (from 1 January 2007) 978 1 84089 427

Printed in China

Imagine you're a
Cowboy!

Lucy Lonestar

was born under a wandering star. She spent her early wild years travelling the prairies and plains on her faithful steed, Lucky. She made a modest living painting pictures and singing in saloons, before hitching her wagon to a trusty cowboy and his rambling ranch.

Mustang Meg

is home from the prairie. Her wagon has finished its journeys and she is corralled in a snug little ranch house where she can gaze at the stars on moonlit nights and think of wide-open spaces and cowboys she has known.

For Cowboy Saul and his band of brothers, Dan, Matt, and Jake.

What is a Cowboy?

Definition:

A cowboy is a man who herds
and looks after cattle

What Do Cowboys Look Like?

There are some cowboys who are chunky and cheerful.

There are some cowboys who are long and lean and quiet.

Cowboys come in many different shapes and sizes
but all cowboys must be able to ride horses.
Cowboy films often show cowboys who are handsome,
clean shaven, young and fair skinned.

In real life cowboys were often quite old. They were covered in
dust and had little time to wash or shave. Usually their horses
were more handsome than they were. Many runaway slaves
could ride horses so there were some black cowboys, too.

The History of Cowboys

Cowboys

Two hundred years ago in North America a huge plain of grasses
covered most of the land. Wild animals and different tribes of
Indians lived there. Herds of buffalo roamed the prairie.
Then settlers came from the east and gradually took more
and more of the land.
They needed meat to eat so herds of cattle came too.
Cowboys were needed to move the herds from one place to another.
This could take months so the cowboys lived and worked
together and became very friendly.

Indians

The original people of America are called Native Americans, and used to be known as Indians. This is because when the first Europeans arrived in America they thought they had reached India. In fact there were many peoples living in that vast land, each with their own customs, language, dress and beliefs. Like many nations living near each other they disagreed and had fights, but the arrival of European settlers created much greater problems. Many small tribes were wiped out. Settlers' families were killed by the war-parties. The great hunting lands were fenced and the herds of buffalo began to disappear. Some of the native inhabitants starved or were forced to change their way of life.

The Wild West

The wagons have stopped and the horses are hitched nearby.
The cowboys can rest and look at the distant mountains, the fish
in the creek and the setting sun.

Sunset

Distant mountains

Horses tied up

Covered wagons

Campfire

Campfire Songs

After a hard day in the saddle, the cowboys light a blazing fire
and cook supper. Then, full of baked beans and under a huge sky
with millions of twinkling stars, they sing their favourite songs.

She'll be coming round the mountain when she comes
She'll be coming round the mountain when she comes
She'll be coming round the mountain, coming round the mountain
Coming round the mountain when she comes

My four-legged friend
My four-legged friend
He'll never let you down
He's honest and faithful right up to the end
My wonderful one, two, three four-legged friend

Horses

Cowboys cannot do their job without horses.
A special bond grows between
a cowboy and his horse.

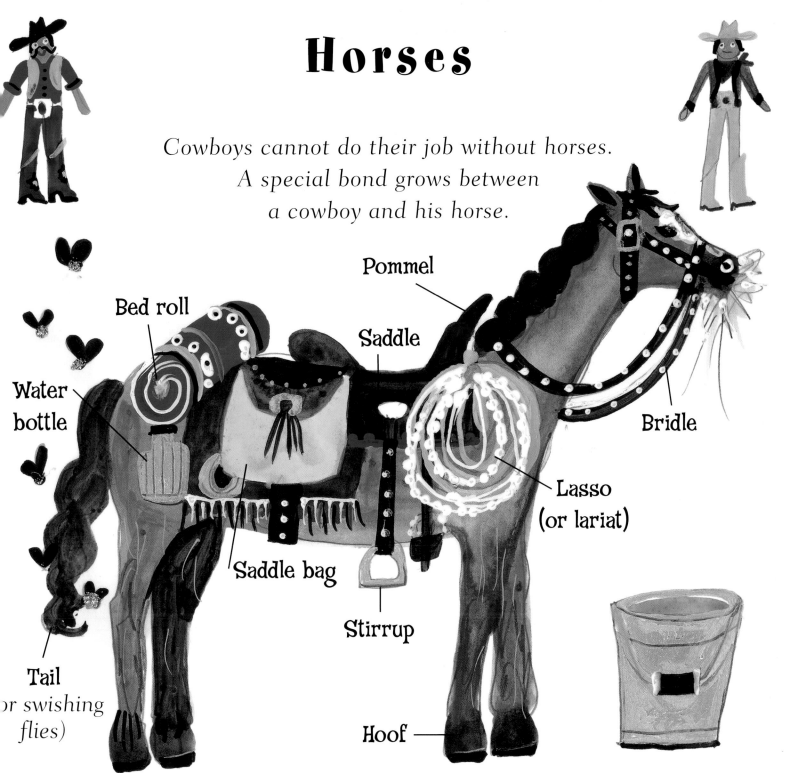

Pommel

Bed roll

Saddle

Water
bottle

Bridle

Lasso
(or lariat)

Saddle bag

Stirrup

Tail
(or swishing
flies)

Hoof

The horse has to carry all this and a cowboy.
Then all he gets at the end of a long day is a handful of hay,
some campfire songs and a mouth organ to listen to.

Rodeos

A rodeo is a cowboy gathering celebrating the skills of a cowboy. It includes a lot of horse riding, competitions for lassoing, trick riding, bucking bronco riding (which is all about cowboys falling off horses), riding bulls and falling off them, and general mayhem. The cowboys wear their best outfits and everyone has a good time and it turns into a party. The cowboys never show when they get hurt because they are rough and tough.

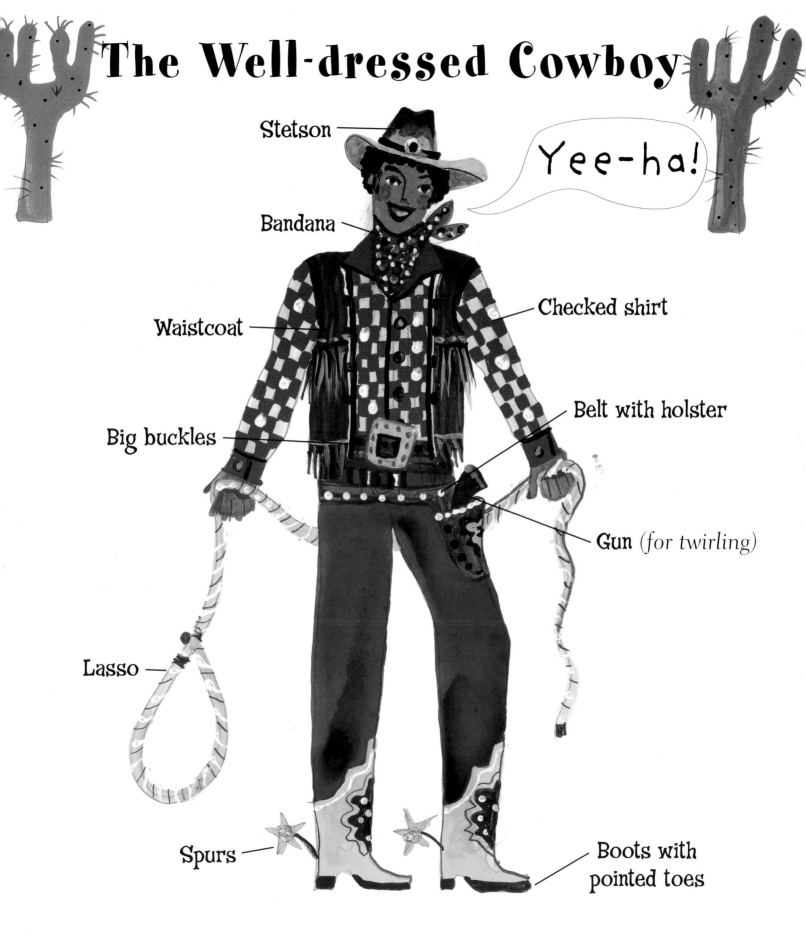

Cowboy Words

Bandana

A scarf that was usually tied around the neck but could be pulled up over the face in dust storms.

Bedroll

Blankets which are rolled up during the day and slung on the back of the saddle until bedtime.

Denims

Trousers made from blue cotton serge from the town in France called Nîmes (de Nîmes).

Chaps

Leather leg protectors.

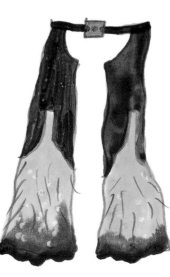

Stetson

A type of hat designed by John Stetson with a high crown and a wide brim to keep sun and rain off the face.

Corral

Fencing which makes an enclosure for steers and horses.

Levi's

Levi Strauss made tough trousers from strong canvas material he originally bought to make into tents.

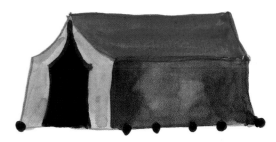

Spurs

Nasty sharp spikes put onto boots. They were jabbed into the horse's side to make it go faster.

Interview with a Cowboy

Prairie Patrick is interviewed by
Daniel Dude for the **Mustang Mirror**.

Prairie Patrick: Howdy

Daniel Dude: Prairie Pat, you are famous as a rodeo star and a rough tough cowboy. Have you always wanted to be a cowboy?

PP: Yup, ever since I were a little bitty kid.

DD: When did you first learn to ride a horse?

PP: When I were a little bitty kid.

DD: When you are out on the range do you lie on your bedroll and think what a lucky man you are?

PP: Yup.

DD: Do you never feel lonely out there in all that space?

PP: Nope

DD: *What is your favourite music?*

PP: *Mouth organ*

DD: *What is your favourite food?*

PP: *Beans*

DD: *Who is your favourite person?*

PP: *Horse. They don't mind the beans.*

DD: *Can you give any advice to anyone who wants to be a cowboy?*

PP: *Waterproof hat. Padded pants. Gotta like horses.*

DD: *Thank you very much Prairie Pat. I can't wait to be a cowboy just like you.*

Cowboy Places

The Ranch

On the ranch there are big barns for storing feed and equipment, stables for the horses, bunk houses for the cowboys and a ranch house where the owner can live. Outside are paddocks and corrals for the animals. Although the cowboys spend a lot of time out on the open plains they know that back at the ranch are all the comforts of home. They can wash their socks and shave their whiskers and sleep on beds instead of prairie grass.

Ghost towns

On the great plains, towns could be built very quickly; perhaps for a team of railway workers, or because gold had been found nearby or because the wagon trains stopped there. However, some of these places became deserted towns with empty streets, boarded-up windows, dusty saloon bars and shadowy forgotten houses. Tumble weeds roll about the crumbling walkways. These are the ghost towns. At daybreak can you hear the galloping of horses and the chatter of the townsfolk? At night can you hear cowboys laughing in the saloon bar and see lamplight flickering in the windows? Or is it just imagination?

The Saloon

Now, although cowboys are mostly rough and tough there are times when they like to relax. If there is one place where a cowboy can relax more than any other it is the saloon in town. In fact, sometimes cowboys become so relaxed that they get roaring drunk and do lots of shooting (which is illegal) and lots of kissing the saloon girls (which is unwise). They end up with sore heads and no pocket money left.

Butch Cassidy and the Sundance Kid

Butch Cassidy and the Sundance Kid were very good at riding horses and herding steers. The trouble was, they were someone else's horses and someone else's steers. Butch Cassidy was the leader of 'The Wild Bunch', a gang of outlaws who rustled cattle and robbed banks, stage coaches and express trains.

He and the Sundance Kid went to South America with a woman called Etta Place and carried out lots of bank robberies. They were kind and generous to those in need. They had many friends. Unfortunately, even kind and friendly people have to obey the law. They didn't – so the law caught them.

Buffalo Bill

William (Bill) Cody was an Indian scout. A journalist came out to the west looking for someone to help him write stories about the Wild West, and Cody helped him. Buffalo Bill Cody became very famous and a show based on his daring adventures was very popular in the United States and Europe – it was called 'The Wild West Show'.

Annie Oakley

Annie Oakley was a wonderful shot with a rifle. She joined the 'Wild West Show' as 'Little Sure Shot'. When the show went to Europe she shot the ash off the end of a cigarette being held in Kaiser Wilhelm of Germany's mouth as a trick. It is a good thing she managed it.

Things to Do

Indian sign language

On the plains were many different Indian nations, each with their own customs and languages. So if they met Indians from another nation, or cowboys, they used sign language or symbols to communicate with each other. Make up a set of secret signs to use with your friends. Here are some you could try:

hand raised with palm forwards = hello   hand raised palm facing you = goodbye

touch nose = I don't like this teacher   touch neck = see you in the playground

Track symbols

When out with your friends make up a set of symbols for tracking.
Use sticks and stones to show which way you have gone.
Use a pile of stones to
indicate danger.

Billy Can Beans

Ask an adult to help you with this.

Into a billy can (or frying pan) put a lump of fat. Fry
chopped onions for 5 minutes. Add sausages and cook
until brown. Add bacon strips and cook on both sides.
Into the pan add a tin of baked beans until they all
sizzle together. This tastes best if you sit cross-legged
outside somewhere. Mop up the juices with bread.
You can still enjoy this if you are a vegetarian cowboy.
Use oil, vegetarian sausages and mushrooms.